D0051120

HEALING THE ADULT CHILD'S
GRIEVING HEART

Sangre de Cristo
Hospice & Palliative Care
In Loving Memory of
Ann Coyle

Also by Alan Wolfelt:

Creating Meaningful Funeral Ceremonies:
A Guide for Families

Healing a Child's Grieving Heart:
100 Practical Ideas for Families,
Friends and Caregivers

Healing a Friend's Grieving Heart:
100 Practical Ideas for Helping Someone
You Love Through Loss

Healing Your Grieving Heart for Kids:
100 Practical Ideas

The Journey Through Grief:
Reflections on Healing

Understanding Your Grief:
Ten Essential Touchstones for Finding
Hope and Healing Your Heart

The Wilderness of Grief: Finding Your Way

Companion Press is dedicated to the education and support of both the bereaved and bereavement caregivers. We believe that those who companion the bereaved by walking with them as they journey in grief have a wondrous opportunity: to help others embrace and grow through grief—and to lead fuller, more deeply-lived lives themselves because of this important ministry.

For a complete catalog and ordering information, write or call:

Companion Press
The Center for Loss and Life Transition
3735 Broken Bow Road
Fort Collins, CO 80526
(970) 226-6050
www.centerforloss.com

HEALING THE ADULT CHILD'S GRIEVING HEART

·

100 PRACTICAL IDEAS AFTER YOUR PARENT DIES

·

ALAN D. WOLFELT, PH.D.

Companion
PRESS

Fort Collins, Colorado

An imprint of the Center for Loss and Life Transition

Companion Press is an imprint of the
Center for Loss and Life Transition,
3735 Broken Bow Road, Fort Collins, Colorado 80526
970-226-6050
www.centerforloss.com

Companion Press books may be purchased in bulk for sales promotions, premiums or fundraisers. Please contact the publisher at the above address for more information.

Printed in the United States of America

12 11 10   5 4 3

ISBN: 978-1-879651-31-9

INTRODUCTION

It was a balmy late summer day in Indiana. My strong, hard-working, yet always loving father lay in a hospital bed recovering from cancer surgery. This powerful man who always seemed in control looked so helpless, so weak, so vulnerable. In a way I felt like I was in a twilight zone, where nothing seemed quite real. And then it hit me like a ton of bricks: My dad, my precious father, my mentor, my protector, was dying.

That night, a night that will always live in my heart, I stayed at my father's side. In the darkness of that hospital room came the light of honoring his many stories of a recalled life. A life lived with sacrifice, integrity, faith, purpose, and most of all, unconditional love.

His love of family flowed out of stories from his childhood. He told me how his mother inspired his love for baseball. He told me how his father was not very emotionally or physically available to him as he grew from childhood to adolescence. He told me of his deep love for his older brothers and sister.

In the midst of my awareness that I would soon not have my father in my life, I listened and I learned. I affirmed that his love for me was true and abiding. I learned of his fears about my mother, who would survive him. I grew acutely aware of what I already knew—my father was a great man, a loving husband and a wonderful father.

My father's memories of his 72 years on earth encouraged me to reflect on my life with him over the last 45 years. The "little things" now had so much more meaning and value to me: playing catch in the backyard; going on our annual camping trip; him teaching me how to drive a manual transmission; washing a car in the driveway together; playing tennis for hours on end; watching him give of his time to his church and his friends; and perhaps most of all, remembering his encouragement and inspiration to me about following my dreams.

I've always thought that accomplishment is inspired by knowing that one is loved. While my dad wasn't always effusive with words of love (after all, he was a German male!), I never doubted his love for me. Yes, my father INSPIRED me.

Honoring my father's many stories that night and recalling my own precious memories of my life with him blessed me with a sacred moment in time. As I helped him prepare to leave the hospital, he gave me a "high five," and with a glint in his eye said, "Thanks for listening. Thanks for helping me make a plan to go home." My terrific father died quietly on November 24, 1999. My heart was turned inside out.

While this book is not about me and my dad, I share some of my story with you to help you embrace some of the many thoughts and feeling you may be experiencing right now.

Each year more than 15 million North Americans experience the death of a parent. For many adult children, it is their last parent. As a matter of fact, by the time we reach age sixty-two, 75 percent of us have lost both parents. Loss of a parent is the single most common form of bereavement in both the United States and Canada.

For the baby boom generation, which makes up one-third of the population of North America, the loss of parents surrounds us.

As one author noted, "Just as baby boomers are beginning to hit their stride, attaining maturity, professional achievement, financial security, and personal peace—WHAM, the wind is knocked out of their sails."

Yes, even if you are in your thirties, forties, fifties, or sixties, you are still your parent's child. No matter how old you are, there are still times when you need your mommy and daddy. The parent-child relationship often serves as a "mirror" that helps reflect who you are in this big world. It only makes sense that the death of a parent leaves you with a broken heart.

Your parent has died, perhaps even your last parent, leaving you an "adult orphan." You are in mourning. You are bereft. To be "bereaved" literally means "to be torn apart" and "to have special needs." The death of your parent calls out to you to honor your special needs right now!

Perhaps your most important "special need" right now is to be compassionate with yourself. The word compassion literally means "with passion." So, self-compassion means caring for oneself "with passion."

While I hope you have excellent outside support, this book is intended to help you be kind to yourself. Over my many years as a grief counselor, walking with people in grief, I have discovered that many of us are hard on ourselves when we are in mourning. We often have inappropriate expectations of how "well" we should be doing with our grief.

These expectations result from common societal messages that tell us to be strong in the face of grief. We may be told to "carry on," to "keep our chins up" and to "be glad we had our parent as long as we did." In actuality, when we are in grief we need to slow down, to turn inward, to embrace our feelings of loss and to seek and accept support. It's not easy to be self-compassionate in our mourning-avoidant culture.

But good self-care is essential to your survival. To practice good self-care doesn't mean you are feeling sorry for yourself; rather it means you are allowing yourself to heal. For it is in nurturing ourselves, in allowing ourselves the time and loving attention we need to journey through our grief, that we find meaning in our continued living. It is in having the courage to care for our own needs that we discover a fullness to our living and loving.

As promised, this book contains 100 practical ideas to help you practice self-compassion as you mourn the death of your parent. Some of the ideas will teach you about the principles of grief and morning. One of the most important ways to help yourself is to learn about the grief experience; the more you know, the less likely you will be to unknowingly perpetuate some of our society's harmful myths about grief and healing.

You'll also notice that each of the 100 ideas suggest a "carpe diem," which means, as fans of the movie "Dead Poets Society" will remember, "seize the day." My hope is that you will not relegate this book to your shelves but keep it handy on your nightstand or desk. Pick it up often and turn to any page; the carpe diem suggestion will help you seize the day by helping you move toward healing today, right now, right this minute. If you come to an idea that doesn't seem to fit you, ignore it and flip to a different page.

I once heard someone say, "We create space for love, and when love leaves, the space remains." As you read this book, I realize the "space" remains. However, I hope these 100 self-care ideas and principles encourage you to nurture yourself in ways that bring hope and healing.

Alan D. Wolfelt

1.

UNDERSTAND THE DIFFERENCE BETWEEN GRIEF AND MOURNING

- Grief is what we think and feel on the inside when someone we love dies.

- Mourning is the outward expression of our grief.

- Everyone grieves when someone loved dies, but if we are to heal, we must also mourn.

- Many of the ideas in this book are intended to help you mourn the death of your parent, to express your grief outside of yourself. Over time and with the support of others, to mourn is to heal.

- Mourning the death of a parent isn't always easy. As a society, we tend to perpetuate the myth that the death of a parent—particularly an elderly parent—is to be expected and should be "gotten over" quickly. So if you express your grief outside yourself, your friends and even your family may not support you.

- If some of your friends and family are not compassionately supporting your need to mourn, seek out the company of those who will.

CARPE DIEM

Ask yourself this: Have I been mourning my parent's death or have I restricted myself to grieving?

2.

BE COMPASSIONATE WITH YOURSELF

- The journey through grief is a long and difficult one. It is also a journey for which there is no preparation.

- For many people today, the death of a parent is the first death they experience among their close loved ones. This unfamiliarity with death and grief can heighten feelings of disbelief and sadness.

- Be compassionate with yourself as you encounter painful thoughts and feelings.

- Don't judge yourself or try to set a particular course for healing. There is no one way to grieve the death of a parent. There is only what you think and feel and the expressing of those thoughts and feelings.

- Let your journey be what it is. And let yourself—your new, grieving self—be who you are.

CARPE DIEM

If you have the energy, take a walk today through a quiet area of town. Or better yet, get out of town and find a "safe place" in nature. Rest when you're tired and contemplate the ways in which you might take better care of yourself in the coming weeks and months.

3.

DON'T EXPECT YOURSELF TO MOURN OR HEAL IN A CERTAIN WAY OR IN A CERTAIN TIME

- Your unique grief journey will be shaped by many factors, including:
    - the nature of the relationship you had with the parent who died.
    - the age of the parent who died.
    - your age.
    - the circumstances of the death.
    - your family's coping and communication styles.
    - your unique personality.
    - your cultural background.
    - your religious or spiritual beliefs.
    - your gender.
    - your support systems.

- Because of these and other factors, no two deaths are ever mourned in precisely the same way. If both of your parents have died, you may find yourself mourning the two deaths in very different ways or similarly.

- Don't have rigid expectations for your thoughts, feelings and behaviors. Instead, celebrate your uniqueness.

CARPE DIEM

Draw two columns on a piece of paper. Title the left column "What I used to think it would be like after my mother/father died." Title the right column "What it's really like." Jot down notes in both columns.

4.

ALLOW FOR NUMBNESS

- Feelings of shock, numbness and disbelief are nature's way of temporarily protecting us from the full reality of the death of someone loved. They help us survive our early grief. I often say, "Thank God for numbness and denial."

- We often think, "I will wake up and this will not have happened." Mourning can feel like being in a dream. The world feels distant, almost unreal—especially the lives of other people. The world turns, but you may not feel it. Time moves, but you may not experience it.

- Your emotions need time to catch up with what your mind has been told. This is true even when death has followed a long illness.

- Even after you have moved beyond these initial feelings, don't be surprised if they reemerge. Birthdays, holidays and anniversaries often trigger these normal and necessary feelings.

CARPE DIEM

If you're feeling numb, cancel any commitments that require concentration and decision-making. Allow yourself time to regroup.

5.

EXPECT TO HAVE A MULTITUDE OF FEELINGS

- Mourners don't just feel sad. We may feel numb, angry, guilty, afraid, confused or even relieved. Sometimes these feelings follow each other within a short period of time or they may occur simultaneously.

- As strange as some of these emotions may seem to you, they are normal and healthy.

- After my father died, I felt the need to try to be "in control," yet I felt out of control. I felt overwhelming sadness, confusion, even some relief that he would no longer struggle as he tried to breathe.

- Allow yourself to feel whatever it is you are feeling without judging yourself.

- Talk about your feelings with someone who cares and can supportively listen.

CARPE DIEM

Which emotion has surprised you most since your parent's death? In your mind, single out this emotion for a moment and give it play. Embrace it. Honor it. And affirm it by talking to someone else who has journeyed through grief after the death of a parent.

6.

BE AWARE THAT YOUR GRIEF AFFECTS YOUR BODY, HEART, SOCIAL SELF AND SPIRIT

- Grief is physically demanding. The body responds to the stress of the encounter and the immune system can weaken. You may be more susceptible to illness and physical discomforts. You may also feel lethargic or highly fatigued. You may not be sleeping well.

- The emotional toll of grief is complex and painful. Mourners often feel many different feelings, and those feelings can shift and blur over time.

- Bereavement naturally results in social discomfort. Friends and family often withdraw from mourners, leaving us isolated and unsupported.

- Mourners often ask ourselves, "Why go on living?" "Will my life have meaning now?" "Where is God in this?" Spiritual questions such as these are natural and necessary but also draining.

- Basically, your grief may affect every aspect of your life. Nothing may feel "normal" right now. If this is true for you, don't be alarmed. Just trust that in time, you will find peace and comfort again.

CARPE DIEM

If you've felt physically affected by your grief, see a doctor this week. Sometimes it's comforting to receive a clean bill of health.

7.

EMBRACE YOUR SPIRITUALITY

- Above all, grief is a journey of the soul. It demands you to consider why people live, why people die and what gives life meaning. These are the most spiritual questions we have language to form.

- Since your parent has died, you've probably found yourself contemplating your own death. This is very common. After all, now that our parents have died, our generation is next in line.

- For many people, formal places of worship—churches, synagogues, mosques—offer a safe place and a ritualized process for discovering and embracing their spirituality. If you don't belong to a place of worship, perhaps now is a good time to join.

- For me, spending time alone in nature provides both the solitude and the beautiful evidence of God's existence that I need to nurture my soul.

- We grow, we learn; the spiritual path is a lifetime unfolding process. The death of your parent often inspires this spiritual unfolding. Make the effort to embrace your spirituality and it will embrace you back by inspiring you with a sense of peace, hope and healing.

CARPE DIEM

Perhaps you have a friend who seems spiritually grounded. Talk to this person about his beliefs and spiritual experiences. Ask him how he learned to nurture his spirituality.

8.

TELL THE STORY, OVER AND OVER AGAIN IF NECESSARY

- Acknowledging a death is a painful, ongoing need that we meet in doses, over time. A vital part of healing in grief is often "telling the story" over and over again.

- The "story" relates the circumstances surrounding the death, reviewing the relationship, describing aspects of the personality of the parent who died, and sharing memories, good and bad.

- It's as if each time we tell the story, it becomes a little more real. It also becomes a more integrated part of who we are.

- Find people who are willing to listen to you tell your story, over and over again if necessary, without judgment..

CARPE DIEM

Tell the story to someone today in the form of a letter. Perhaps you can write and send this letter to a friend who lives far away. If you are not a letter writer, find a trusted friend to "talk out" the story. You will know who will be willing to listen and who won't.

9.

HELP ERADICATE THE MYTH THAT ADULT CHILDREN NEEDN'T MOURN WHEN A PARENT DIES

- Here's how the myth goes: Everybody dies. People who have lived a long, full life are expected to die. You're a grown-up; you know these things. You shouldn't be so upset when your parent dies.

- But the death of someone you love, especially someone who played such a big part in your life, is a profound loss. Whether your parent was very old or middle-aged, whether the death was sudden or anticipated, someone you loved and who loved you will never be physically present to you again. Of course you grieve! Of course you need to mourn!

- I find that other adults who've experienced the death of a parent are often empathetic. They've encountered this myth, too, and found it to be totally counter to their experience.

- When the opportunity arises, let others know that the death of a parent is not easy. Expressing your thoughts and feelings will help your community know that grief is timeless and ageless.

CARPE DIEM

If you have a friend whose parent died, talk about this experience. Ask: What was it like for you when your mother or father died? She may welcome the opportunity to express her thoughts and feelings and you may be comforted by the knowledge that you're not alone.

10.

MOVE TOWARD YOUR GRIEF, NOT AWAY FROM IT

- Our society teaches us that emotional pain is to be avoided, not embraced, yet it is only in moving toward our grief that we can be healed.

- As Helen Keller once said, "The only way to get to the other side is to go through the door."

- Note that the phrase "move toward your grief" invites you to take an active role in your healing. Don't think of yourself as a powerless victim or as helpless in the face of grief. Instead, empower yourself to "do something" with your grief—to mourn it, to express it outside yourself, to find ways to help yourself heal.

- Be suspicious if you find yourself thinking that you're "doing well" since the death. Sometimes "doing well" means you're avoiding your pain.

CARPE DIEM

Today, do something to confront and express your grief. Maybe it's time to tell someone close to you how you've really been feeling.

11.

REVIEW YOUR RELATIONSHIP
WITH THE PARENT WHO DIED

- One way to mourn your parent's death is to think through, write and talk about your relationship with your parent. How did your parent treat you? What words would your parent use to describe you? What did your parent value about you?

- Also think about your feelings for your parent and why those feelings were most prominent. What was your parent like? How did you respond to your parent? How did your parent shape you?

- What was your role in your family? Were you the "smart one" or the "funny one" or the "troublemaker" or the "peacemaker?" How did your role affect your relationship with this parent? How do you feel about this role now that you're an adult?

- I shared a fairly dry sense of humor with my father. At times we would laugh at something that others in our presence wouldn't understand. I miss that! What do you miss that you shared with your parent?

- Ultimately, thinking through these kinds of questions and talking or writing about them may help you reconcile ambivalent feelings and old hurts. You may achieve a sense of peace about your parent and the life the two of you lived side by side.

CARPE DIEM

On a large piece of paper, draw a timeline of your life. Write in significant events and dates. Also write in significant events and dates in the life of your parent. How did your two lives connect? How did your life affect your parent's and vice versa?

12.

ACKNOWLEDGE ALL THE LOSSES THIS DEATH HAS WROUGHT

- When a parent dies, you lose not only the physical presence of your parent, but also a part of your self—that part that your parents gave life to and loved and nurtured.

- One of the most difficult losses for grieving adult children can be the loss of acceptance and affirmation. As you continue to achieve and grow in life, your parent will no longer be there to give you her blessing.

- When your parent dies, you may also lose the house you have always thought of as home and the connection to the town you grew up in.

- If you have children of your own, you may also mourn the grandparents they will no longer have and the sense of Family with a capital F that your parents tacitly brought to any gathering.

- Allowing yourself to acknowledge the many levels of loss the death has brought to your life will help you move forward in your grief journey.

CARPE DIEM

Name the things that you've lost or events you'll mourn
in the future as a result of your parent's death.

13.

ALLOW FOR FEELINGS OF
UNFINISHED BUSINESS

- The death of a parent often brings about feelings of unfinished business. Things we never did, things we didn't get to say, things we wish we hadn't.

- Allow yourself to think and feel through these "if onlys" and "should haves." You may never be able to fully resolve these issues, but if you permit yourself to mourn them, you will be become reconciled to them.

- Is there something you wanted to say to your parent but never did? Write her a letter that openly expresses your thoughts and feelings—but only when you're ready. Or, it may be more natural for you to "talk out" these things with a trusted friend or counselor.

- Talk with your siblings or your spouse about these feelings. Your siblings probably have similar regrets of their own. Sharing them with each other may help you reconcile them.

CARPE DIEM

Take this opportunity to tie up any loose ends you
may have with someone who's still alive. Express
your feelings and renew your relationship.

14.

REACH OUT TO OTHERS FOR HELP

- Perhaps the most compassionate thing you can do for yourself at this difficult time is to reach out for help from others.

- Think of it this way: Grieving may be the hardest work you have ever done. And hard work is less burdensome when others lend a hand. Life's greatest challenges—getting through school, raising children, pursuing a career—are in many ways team efforts. So it should be with mourning.

- Sharing your pain with others won't make it disappear, but it will, over time, make it more bearable. I have found it particularly helpful to talk to other adult children who have experienced the death of a parent. From our common bond comes hope for our mutual healing.

- Reaching out for help also connects you to other people and strengthens the bonds of love that make life seem worth living again.

CARPE DIEM

Call a close friend who may have distanced himself from you since the death and tell him how much you need him right now. Suggest specific ways he can help.

15.

IDENTIFY THREE PEOPLE
YOU CAN TURN TO ANYTIME
YOU NEED A FRIEND

- You may have many people who care about you but few who are able to be good companions in grief.

- Identify three people whom you think can be there for you in the coming weeks and months.

- Don't assume that others will help. Even normally compassionate people sometimes find it hard to be present to others in grief.

- I find that after a death, you can usually divide the people you know into three groups. The neutral group won't harm you in your grief, nor will they generally be of much help. The harmful group will make you feel worse by what they say or do. And the helpful group will be available to you and supportive of your need to mourn. Try to spend time with those who help and set boundaries with those who are harmful to you right now.

CARPE DIEM

Call the three people you've identified and ask them outright:
Are you willing to help me with my grief? Tell them you mainly
need to spend time with them and talk to them freely.

16.

UNDERSTAND THE SIX NEEDS OF MOURNING

Need #1: Acknowledge the reality of the death.

- This first need of mourning requires you to gently confront the difficult reality that your parent is dead and will never physically be present to you again.

- Whether the death was sudden or anticipated, acknowledging the full reality of the loss may occur over weeks and months.

- You will first acknowledge the reality of the loss with your head. Only over time will you come to acknowledge it with your heart.

- At times you may push away the reality of your parent's death. This is normal. You will come to integrate the reality, in doses, as you are ready.

CARPE DIEM

Tell someone about the death today. You might talk
about the circumstances of the death or review the
relationship you had with your mother or father. Talking
about it will help you work on this important need.

17.

UNDERSTAND THE SIX NEEDS OF MOURNING

Need #2: Embrace the pain of the loss.

• This need requires mourners to embrace the pain of their loss—something we naturally don't want to do. It is easier to avoid, repress or push away the pain of grief than it is to confront it.

• It is in embracing your grief, however, that you will learn to reconcile yourself to it.

• Always remember that your pain is normal and necessary. You are not being "overly emotional" if you feel devastated after the death of a parent. You are not being childish. You are not weak or immature. The bond between parent and child runs very deep, and its history tells, in large part, the story of who you are. Even if your parent "lived a good life" or was old or sick, the death may well feel like a very profound loss to you. No matter how old you are or how old your parent was, you are still and always that parent's child.

• You will probably need to "dose" yourself in embracing your pain. If you were to allow in all the pain at once, you could not survive.

CARPE DIEM

If you feel up to it, allow yourself a time for embracing pain today. Dedicate 15 minutes to thinking about and feeling the loss. Reach out to someone who doesn't try to take your pain away and spend some time with him.

18.

UNDERSTAND THE SIX NEEDS OF MOURNING

Need #3: Remember the parent who died.

• When someone loved dies, they live on in us through memory.

• To heal, you need to actively remember the parent who died and commemorate the life that was lived.

• Never let anyone take your memories away in a misguided attempt to save you from pain. It's good for you to continue to display photos of your mother or father. It's good for you to talk about your parent's life and death. It's good for you to hold onto objects that belonged to your mother or father.

• Remembering the past makes hoping for the future possible. As E.M. Forster wrote, "Unless we remember we cannot understand." And, as Kierkegaard noted, "Life is lived forward but understood backward."

CARPE DIEM

Brainstorm a list of characteristics or memories of your parent. Write as fast as you can for 10 minutes (or more), then put away your list for later reflection.

19.

UNDERSTAND THE SIX NEEDS OF MOURNING

Need #4: Develop a new self-identity

• A large part of your self-identity was formed by the relationship you had with the parent who died. For your entire life, you have been the son or daughter of your parent. You have been a member of your family of origin.

• Now you are motherless or fatherless. If both parents have died, you may feel "orphaned." The way you defined yourself and the way society defines you is changed.

• Adult children who have been "orphaned" often feel burdened by the sense that they are now the matriarchs or patriarchs of the family. They are now the "grown-ups." And now, no generation stands between them and death.

• You need to re-anchor yourself, to reconstruct your self-identity. This is arduous and painful work.

• Many mourners discover that as they work on this need, they ultimately discover some positive changes, such as becoming more caring or less judgmental.

CARPE DIEM

Write out a response to this prompt: I used to be _____.
Now that _____ died, I am _____. This makes me
feel _____. Keep writing as long as you want.

20.

UNDERSTAND THE SIX NEEDS OF MOURNING

Need #5: Search for meaning.

- When someone we love dies, we naturally question the meaning and purpose of life and death.

- "Why?" questions may surface uncontrollably and often precede "How" questions. Questions such as "Why did my mother die this way?" or "Why did my father have to get sick?" often come before "How will I go on living?"

- You will probably question your philosophy of life and explore religious and spiritual values as you work on this need.

- Remember that having faith or spirituality does not negate your need to mourn. Even if you believe in life after death or that your parent has gone to "a better place," you still have the right and the need to mourn this significant loss in your life. "Blessed are those who mourn for they shall be comforted."

CARPE DIEM

Write down a list of "why" questions that may have surfaced for you since the death. Find a friend or counselor who will explore these questions with you without thinking she has to give you answers.

21.

UNDERSTAND THE SIX
NEEDS OF MOURNING

Need #6: Receive ongoing support from others.

• As mourners, we need the love and understanding of others if we are
  to heal.

• If you feel dependent on others right now, don't feel ashamed.
  Instead, revel in the knowledge that others care about you.
  Acknowledging your need for support is not a weakness, it is
  a strength.

• Unfortunately, our society places too much value on "carrying on"
  and "doing well" after a death—especially after the death of an
  elderly parent. So, many grieving adult children are abandoned by
  their friends and family soon after the death.

• Grief is a process, not an event, and you will need the continued
  support of your friends and family for weeks, months and years.

CARPE DIEM

Sometimes your friends want to support you but don't know
how. Ask. Call your closest friend right now and tell her you
need her help through the coming weeks and months.

22.

KNOW THAT GRIEF DOES NOT PROCEED IN ORDERLY, PREDICTABLE "STAGES"

- Though the "Needs of Mourning" (Ideas 16-21) are numbered 1-6, grief is not an orderly progression towards healing. Don't fall into the trap of thinking your grief journey will be predictable or always forward-moving.

- Usually, grief hurts more before it hurts less.

- You will probably experience a multitude of different emotions in a wave-like fashion. You will also likely encounter more than one need of mourning at the same time.

- Be compassionate with yourself as you experience your own unique grief journey.

CARPE DIEM

Has anyone told you that you are in this or that "stage" of grief? Ignore this usually well-intended advice. Don't allow yourself or anyone else to compartmentalize your grief.

23.

IF ONE OF YOUR PARENTS HAS DIED, CONSIDER THIS

- The death of a parent seems always to be a shock, whether the death was sudden or anticipated. Your parent was and always will be one of the central figures, the most important people, in your life. Even parents who were absent from their children's lives play a large psychological and emotional role.

- If your parent was the first significant person in your life to die, you may find yourself encountering grief and the harsh realities of death for the first time. This is never easy.

- What do parents represent? They are a stabilizing presence; they are keepers of our history and childhood; they are our connection to the past; they are our cheerleaders; they are our most profound source of acceptance and unconditional love. When a parent dies, then, all of these things are torn at the seams.

- Now that one of your parents has died, perhaps you can use your newfound perspective to strengthen your relationship with your surviving parent. How much time might the two of you have left together?

CARPE DIEM

Choose a gift for your surviving parent today. Try to find something emotionally resonant—not necessarily expensive or practical. Wrap it with care and include a note telling him how you feel about him. Bring or ship him the gift as soon as possible.

24.

BE COMPASSIONATE WITH YOUR SURVIVING PARENT

- Your surviving parent will have his or her own needs, of course. Spouses—especially those who have been married for many years—develop complex relationships. Their ways of relating to one another and to the outside world may have taken a lifetime to shape. Now that one of them is gone, the other may seem adrift and incapacitated. Or, the surviving parent may seem remarkably resilient—even relieved—after the death.

- You cannot fill in for the parent who died, but you can be understanding about whatever difficulties your surviving parent may be having. Just as your grief is normal and necessary, so is your surviving parent's.

- If your surviving parent needs more help than you can give, seek out additional helpers. Talk to your siblings, relatives and family friends about sharing responsibilities. Most are more than happy to help if they're given a specific task or role. And talk to your surviving parent, too. You may be surprised at how helpful such a discussion can be.

- Sometimes adult children secretly feel that the "wrong" parent has died. Perhaps the parent you were closer to has died first, or the younger parent or the one who seemed in better health. These feelings are normal and do not indicate a lack of love or compassion, though you may want to explore them further by journaling them or discussing them with someone you trust.

- If your surviving parent cultivates a new love interest, you and your family may have a hard time accepting it. Many intertwined issues arise here, but try to remember that your surviving parent's happiness is most important. Perhaps you can think of this person as adding love to the remainder of your parent's life instead of as a "replacement." Open, gentle communication—no hateful blaming—is the best solution.

CARPE DIEM

Write, call or visit your surviving parent today. For this one day, concentrate on practicing active empathy—understanding your parent's grief experience from his or her perspective.

25.

IF BOTH OF YOUR PARENTS HAVE DIED, CONSIDER THIS

- After both parents have died, many adult children feel incredibly alone—even if they have siblings and families of their own. They often say they feel "orphaned."

- While nobody's parents are perfect, a parent's love is, most of the time, the purest and the most unconditional love we imperfect human beings can muster. Now that your parents are gone, you may feel that no one will love you this deeply again or that you cannot depend on anyone in the same way.

- Once both parents have died, you may no longer have a "home" to go back to. Your sense of rootedness and belonging to a particular place and a particular set of people is severed. Even when you do go "home," it is never the same without your parents.

- While your parents were alive, they were the elder generation. They bore the burdens of age—wisdom, responsibility, physical decline. Now that your parents are dead, you are the elder generation. Confronting aging and mortality can be extremely difficult.

- At bottom, you may feel a loss of control after both of your parents have died. What small changes can you make in your life to help regain some sense of control? Are you living your day-to-day life in alignment with your values and beliefs? What are your talents and gifts?

- If we can give and receive love, we can figure out a place for ourselves in the world, for we can and will create a new home.

CARPE DIEM

Make a list of the things you would like to do before you die. Spend some time ordering these things from most important to least. Take one step today towards working on your most important goal.

26.

IF YOUR FATHER HAS DIED, CONSIDER THIS

- Your response to your father's death will be affected by many factors, including the closeness of your relationship, your age and your father's age, your unique personality and more. But in general, the death of a father seems to cause adult children to feel insecure and ungrounded.

- Historically, fathers have been the authority figures in the family—the wage earners, the decision-makers, the disciplinarians. Because this has changed radically in the past several decades, your father may have played any number of roles in your life. Was your father emotionally reserved or open? Was he a good communicator? Was he there for you? How do your answers to these questions affect your grief?

- Daughters who have lived their lives adored as "Daddy's little girl" may feel a deep loss of love and acceptance when their fathers die. Sons who emulated their fathers or strived to please them may feel a loss of self-worth or purpose.

- As I noted in the Introduction, my father inspired me. Oh, he had his faults (occasional temper outbursts, sometimes he punished instead of disciplining, he was tight with a dollar—and proud of it to a fault!), but at bottom he was a great man, a loving husband and a wonderful father. Actually, I always felt emotionally and spiritually closer to him than to my mother; he was my "safe place."

CARPE DIEM

This Father's Day, do something in honor of your father. Build a birdhouse or dig a new garden. Don't let the day pass without making such an effort.

27.

IF YOUR MOTHER HAS DIED, CONSIDER THIS

- Our mothers gave us life. They bore us and most often raised us, feeding us and dressing us day in and day out when we were very young and continuing as our caretakers as we grew. Who did you turn to when you were hurt? Who best read the flicker of emotion as it crossed your face? Who kissed you and hugged you and made you feel loved?

- If your mother was your primary caregiver when you were a child, you may feel an especially profound sense of loss when she dies. It's as if the person who loved you the most, who understood you the best, who most wanted you to be happy, is now gone.

- Not all mothers play this role, however. If your mother was emotionally distant or absent from your childhood, you may feel angry or regretful. You may mourn less the mother you had and more the mother you wish you had had.

- Consider who your mother was as a person apart from you. What was she like? What did she love? Whom did she touch? Thinking about your mother in this way may give you some comfort and peace.

CARPE DIEM

This Mother's Day, do something in honor of your mother. Bring her favorite flowers to her grave or volunteer for a cause that she supported. Don't let the day pass without making such an effort.

28.

IF YOUR PARENT DIED AFTER AN EXTENDED ILLNESS OR DECLINE, KNOW THAT FEELINGS OF RELIEF ARE PERFECTLY NORMAL

- Due to today's medical advances, people are living much longer than they did in past centuries. Sometimes, modern medicines and machines keep people alive to enjoy life for many extra years. But those same medicines and machines can also prolong illnesses and suffering.

- If your parent died after an extended illness or decline, what you may feel above all else is a tremendous sense of relief. If you cared for or spent time with your parent while he suffered, you may even have wished—prayed!—for a swift death.

- Feelings of relief after a prolonged or painful illness is ended by death are very common. It is perfectly normal and understandable to want your parent's suffering to end and your life to return to normal. A few days before my dad died, he said to me, "This is no way to live…I'm ready." When he died I felt relief in combination with overwhelming sadness.

- Of course, you've probably found that your life is not "normal" anymore. Your parent has died. Your life is forever changed. And even though you were anticipating the death, you may still feel shocked when it actually happens. No one is ever really prepared for the death of someone loved.

- If the death was recent, you may be worried if all you can seem to remember or think about is your parent's suffering and death. Rest assured that in time, you will once again recall happier, gentler memories.

CARPE DIEM

Call or write a note to someone else who was involved in your parent's care during the last days or weeks. Share your feelings with this person and thank her for her concern and help.

29.

IF YOU HELPED CARE FOR YOUR SICK PARENT, GIVE YOURSELF TIME TO RECUPERATE

- Many adult children are surprised to find themselves taking care of their ill or declining parents. Suddenly they feel like the parent and the parent seems like the child.

- This sort of role reversal is emotionally and spiritually draining. You may have felt "sandwiched" between two generations in need of your care: your parents and your own children. Your marriage may have suffered. Your work may have been affected.

- Caring for a sick parent can also be physically draining. You may be exhausted.

- When a parent you have been caring for dies, you may feel gratified that you "did everything you could" or you may feel a sense of failure. You may not know what do with yourself now that your days are no longer consumed by caring for your parent. You may feel a sense of loss now that you are no longer needed.

- Your life changed when your parent became ill and it has changed again now that your parent has died. Give yourself some time and space to absorb this change. Concentrate on caring for yourself right now.

CARPE DIEM

This weekend or one weekend soon, schedule nothing. Plan to putter around the house, sleep, watch movies, read books. Rest your body and your mind and your soul.

30.

IF YOUR PARENT DIED SUDDENLY, LOOK FOR WAYS TO EMBRACE THE REALITY OF THE DEATH

- The sudden death of a parent, like any sudden death, comes as a shock. For a while, the death may seem completely unreal and dreamlike. You may feel as if your parent will phone you or walk through your door at any moment.

- This heightened sense of disbelief protects you in the early days and weeks after the death. If your mind were to force you to confront the reality all at once, you could not survive.

- But later, as you are ready, confronting the reality of the death in doses will help you heal. Encourage yourself to talk about the death. Look at photos of the parent who died. Visit the place of the death and/or your parent's home. Talk with the last people to speak with your parent.

- Embracing the reality of the death can be painful, but even more painful in the long run is pushing it away. To come to terms with this sudden death is to come to terms with continued life.

CARPE DIEM

If your parent died suddenly, close your eyes and imagine your parent's last days or hours. What was she doing when she died? What was the weather like? What were you doing? What thoughts or words would you have conveyed to her at that moment if you could have?

31.

IF YOUR PARENT WAS ABUSIVE, ALLOW YOURSELF TO FEEL AMBIVALENT OR RELIEVED

- Children of abusive parents, whether the abuse was emotional, physical or sexual, often feel a profound sense of relief when the parent dies. Now, finally, the parent can no longer harm the child—even if the child has long since grown up and moved away. Feeling relieved at the death of an abusive parent is normal and understandable.

- In these situations, feelings of regret and rage also often surface— regret that the parent wasn't a better parent, rage that the abuse happened in the first place.

- While you cannot change your childhood, you can help other children who may be victims of abuse. Consider volunteering at your local women's shelter, crisis hotline or victim's advocacy group. You have the power to make a difference in the life of a child—and at the same time, help yourself heal.

CARPE DIEM

If you were abused as child, consider seeking professional therapy. The death of your parent may bring up all kinds of thoughts and feelings that you've been repressing your whole life. Now is the time to explore them with someone you trust.

32.

ACCEPT DIFFERENT GRIEF RESPONSES AMONG SIBLINGS

- Just as there is no one right way for you to mourn, there is no one right way for your brothers and sisters to mourn. You are likely to find that each of your parent's children will mourn the death in markedly different ways.

- The building block of our life is our own singularity. Even when we are kin, we are all individually stamped. Our personalities are as unique as fingerprints.

- While you might have anticipated some of your sibling's responses since the death (for example, your emotional sister has probably always been emotional), other responses may have surprised you. Your brother, whom you thought was emotionally detached, may be a basket-case. Or your conscientious sister may have refused to help plan the funeral. Try not to let these differences alarm you or hurt your feelings. Try to remember that each adult child is doing the best that he or she can at any given moment.

- If there is a surviving parent, each sibling will also relate uniquely to him or her. Try to discuss caregiving responsibilities proactively and vent grievances without blame.

- Usually, discussing differences openly and honestly will help everyone understand and support each other. Perhaps you can be the one to open the dialogue and to make an effort to communicate. If one of your siblings refuses to communicate, know that you did what you could and leave it at that.

CARPE DIEM

If you haven't talked to your siblings recently, call them today. Tell them you've been thinking about them. Ask them how they've been doing since your parent's death. Ask them how their lives have changed. You might be surprised by their answers.

33.

WORK ON YOUR RELATIONSHIP WITH YOUR SIBLINGS

- Sibling relationships are almost always complex and can be difficult to nurture once a parent has died. Sometimes it's as if the glue that held the family together has disintegrated and now new bonds must be formed. Sometimes disagreements or resentments about the parent's care, burial or belongings linger for months and years.

- But you and your siblings share so very much, including the ability to help each other heal. You shared your young lives. You shared your parents. And now you are sharing the loss of a parent. Who could better understand and support each other after a parent dies?

- Times of illness and death are always stressful. If you and your siblings aren't getting along right now, wait a month or two for feelings to soften then try again. In the meantime, try not to say or do anything you'll regret later.

- Ask a family friend or trusted relative to intervene if sibling conflicts are destroying your family. Remember that the goal isn't to place blame but rather to foster harmony.

- Sometimes, no matter what you do to reach out to a sibling, you will be rejected. If this happens, remember—you are responsible *to* your siblings, not *for* them.

CARPE DIEM

Call your sibling today and ask how she's doing. Arrange to meet and spend some leisure time together soon.

34.

NURTURE YOUR RELATIONSHIPS WITH YOUR SPOUSE AND CHILDREN

- Times of illness and death are stressful for everyone involved. Your parent's death—and your reaction to it—has affected many people, including your spouse and your children.

- Have you been open with your partner and children about the effect this death has had on you? Have you communicated your grief? Have you talked to them about theirs?

- If your family hasn't been doing such a good job of openly mourning this death, it's not too late to start. Arrange some quiet time with your spouse and tell him how you've been feeling. Schedule a family meeting and ask everyone to share their feelings about the death.

- You've probably learned many things from your parent's death—what it means to love your family, what's truly important to you, how life should be lived. Now's the time to translate these lessons into action.

CARPE DIEM

Today, surprise your partner with flowers or a small gift.
Tell her how much you love her and how grateful you
were to have her by your side when your parent died.

35.

IF YOU ARE ANGRY, FIND APPROPRIATE WAYS TO EXPRESS YOUR ANGER

- For some grieving adult children, feelings of shock and disbelief after the death are followed by anger.

- You may be angry at medical caregivers, your siblings, your family, your spouse, even your parent.

- Maybe you believe one of your siblings behaved inappropriately. Maybe one of your relatives said something unconscionable. Maybe your spouse has been unsupportive.

- Feelings of anger at the parent who died are quite common. Perhaps you're angry that he didn't quit smoking or didn't see the doctor sooner. Or maybe he left behind a financial or legal mess that you now have to clean up.

- Anger is normal and necessary. It's our way of protesting a reality we don't like. It helps us survive. And anger is far sounder than a resignation to despair. Anger and feelings of protest challenge relationships, where despair severs or cuts off relationships. Anger may be frightening, but indifference is deadening.

CARPE DIEM

Today, do something physical to vent your anger. Go for a fast walk or punch a boxing bag. Smash a tennis ball against a practice wall over and over.

36.

IF YOU ARE UPSET ABOUT THE MEDICAL CARE YOUR PARENT RECEIVED, EXPRESS THOSE FEELINGS

- The modern medical system can be exasperating for patients and their families. If your parent was ill before she died, she may have endured countless doctor visit, tests, diagnoses and treatments.

- But in the end, modern medicine was not able to "cure" your parent. You may feel frustrated that the treatments didn't work. You may feel angry at busy doctors, who perhaps seemed brusque or unthorough. You may feel bad decisions were made. You may feel your parent suffered too much or too long.

- If you harbor bad feelings about your parent's medical care, find a way to express those feelings. I'm not talking about frivolous lawsuits here. I'm simply suggesting that talking out your grievances about your parent's medical care may help you move beyond them to the real work of mourning the death itself.

- Write a letter to the doctor or practice or hospital expressing your concerns, even if you never send it. Do you personally know someone in the medical field? Talk to this person about your feelings; he may be able to provide some "inside" perspective. Or talk out your feelings with your family.

CARPE DIEM

While you may feel upset about some aspect of your parent's care, you probably feel grateful about another. Write a note of thanks to a caregiver who was particularly compassionate or helpful.

37.

IF THERE ARE ESTATE CONFLICTS, RISE ABOVE THE FRAY

- Sometimes after both parents have died, adult children (and sometimes surviving stepparents) squabble over financial matters. Unfortunately, it is not unusual for there to be disagreements and even bitter arguments about who gets what.

- Estate conflicts can ruin relationships among siblings. They also tend to focus emotional energies on money rather than on the loss of the parent who died.

- If your family is embroiled in estate conflicts—whether over a large fortune or a few simple belongings, you can choose to be the peacemaker. Ask yourself: What is really important to me here? At the end of my life, what will matter most? Am I confusing emotional issues with financial ones?

- Sometimes long-suppressed feelings get in the way of honest communication. For example, you may feel that your sister has always been spoiled and now you deserve the lion's share of the estate. Or you may feel that since you took care of your mother while she was ill, you need to be compensated. Express these feelings. Saying them out loud may help you and your family understand what it is you really want.

- Don't let the estate process dominate the mourning process.

CARPE DIEM

Call a meeting (or arrange a conference call) for your siblings to discuss estate conflicts. If you can't be the mediator, appoint someone who can be. The goal of this meeting is to express feelings and calmly discuss varying viewpoints. Be honest and direct without blaming.

38.

DO WHAT FEELS RIGHT WITH YOUR PARENT'S BELONGINGS

- Knowing what to do with their parent's belongings can be a particularly difficult decision for grieving children.

- As with all things in grief, there is no one right way to handle this issue. You must do what feels right for you and your family.

- Ask your siblings or a friend of the family to help you. This is often too large—and too emotional—a task to handle alone.

- When you're ready to sort through your parent's belongings (and do go slowly; there are no rewards for speed!), consider which items might be meaningful later on to you or to others. Don't dispose of things in haste; you won't be able to get them back later.

- If more than one family member requests the same item, those family members should talk to each other about the dispute. For example, maybe your sister always cherished Mom's ring. When people speak honestly and calmly about such matters, often a reasonable and loving agreement can be reached.

- Do keep at least a box of special items just for yourself.

CARPE DIEM

Bring some of the smaller special items that belonged to your parent into a frame shop and ask for help in creating a shadow box.

39.

RELEASE ANY BAD FEELINGS OR REGRETS YOU MAY HAVE ABOUT THE FUNERAL AND BURIAL

- The funeral is a wonderful means of expressing our beliefs, thoughts and feelings about the death of someone loved.

- Funerals help us acknowledge the reality of the death, give testimony to the life of the person who died, express our grief, support each other, and embrace our faith and beliefs about life and death

- Yet for many mourners, funeral planning is difficult. Funeral and burial decisions may have been made quickly, while you were still in deep shock and disbelief. Sometimes some of these decisions seem wrong with the benefit of hindsight.

- If you harbor any negative feelings about your parent's funeral or memorial service, know this: You and everyone else who was a part of the service did the best they could do at the time. You cannot change what happened, but you can talk about what happened and share your thoughts and feelings with someone who cares. Don't berate yourself.

- It's never too late to hold another memorial service for your parent. Perhaps a tree-planting ceremony or a small gathering on the anniversary of the parent's death could be a forum for sharing memories and prayer. Ask a clergyperson or someone you know to be a good public speaker to help plan and lead the ceremony.

CARPE DIEM

If you harbor regrets or anger about your parent's funeral and burial, talk about these feelings with someone today. Perhaps the two of you together can create an "action plan" to help make things better.

40.

PREPARE YOUR CHILDREN FOR YOUR OWN EVENTUAL DEATH

- As a society, we're not very good at death. We don't like to think about it, we don't like to talk about it, and we certainly don't like to plan for it. But now you know: parents die and children grieve.

- How can you prepare your children for their own eventual grief? One way is to give them the best memories that you possibly can. Spend time with them. Accept them for who they are. Love them without condition. And tell them, over and over, how much they mean to you.

- Be open with your children about your grief over your parent's death. Model healthy mourning. Tell them stories from your childhood. Reveal old secrets. Teach them the lessons your parent taught you. Ground them in your faith and your love.

- My three children have witnessed my "griefbursts" since the death of their grandpa. When they miss him, they bring him up and we talk about him. I'm the model for their willingness to openly mourn.

- Consider pre-planning your funeral. While funerals are for the living and shouldn't be rigidly pre-planned, it might help your children to know whether you'd prefer to be buried or cremated and where your remains should be buried or scattered. You might also write down a few suggestions about music you find meaningful or old friends to notify.

CARPE DIEM

Write a note to each of your children telling them how special they are to you and relating good memories. Seal the notes in individual envelopes marked with each child's name. Place the notes with your will or other important papers. Someday—perhaps years or decades from now—your children will find and cherish these loving messages.

41.

CRY

- Tears are a natural cleansing and healing mechanism. It's OK to cry. In fact, it's good to cry when you feel like it. What's more, tears are a form of mourning. They are sacred!

- On the other hand, don't feel bad if you aren't crying a lot. Not everyone is a crier.

- You may find that those around you are uncomfortable with your tears. As a society, we're often not so good at witnessing others in pain.

- Explain to your friends and family that you need to cry right now and that they can help by allowing you to.

- You may find yourself crying at unexpected times or places. If you need to, excuse yourself and retreat to somewhere private. But don't feel shame; you are entitled to your tears.

CARPE DIEM

If you feel like it, have a good cry today. Find a safe place to embrace your pain and cry as long and as hard as you want to.

42.

REACH OUT AND TOUCH

- For many people, physical contact with another human being is healing. It has been recognized since ancient times as having transformative, healing powers.

- When you were a child, did your parent embrace you? Do you remember what it felt like to be safe in the arms of your loving mother or father? While you can't duplicate this precise feeling, reaching out and touching others you love may make you feel better.

- Have you hugged anyone lately? Held someone's hand? Put your arm around another human being?

- You probably know several people who enjoy hugging or physical touching. If you're comfortable with their touch, encourage it in the weeks and months to come.

- Hug someone you feel safe with. Kiss your children or a friend's baby. Walk arm in arm with a neighbor.

- You may want to listen to the song titled "I Know What Love Is," by Don White. I have found this song helps me reflect on how my father held me as a child. Listen to this song then drop me a note or e-mail (DrWolfelt@centerforloss.com) and let me know how it makes you think, and more important, feel.

CARPE DIEM

Try hugging your close friends and family members today,
even if you usually don't. You just might like it!

43.

WRITE A LETTER

- Sometimes articulating our thoughts and feelings in letter-form helps us understand them better.

- Write a letter to the parent who died telling him or her how you feel now. Consider the following prompts:

  - What I miss most about you is . . .
  - What I wish I'd said or hadn't said is . . .
  - What I remember best about you when I was growing up is...
  - What's hardest for me now is . . .
  - What I'd like to ask you is . . .
  - I'm keeping my memories of you alive by . . .
  - Read your letter aloud at the cemetery or to a trusted friend.

- Write a letter to God telling him how you feel about the death.

- Write thank you notes to helpers such as hospice staff, neighbors, doctors, funeral directors, etc.

CARPE DIEM

Write a letter to someone you love who's still alive telling her why she's so important to you. Such letters become treasured keepsakes.

44.

BE MINDFUL OF ANNIVERSARIES

- Anniversaries—of the death, life events, birthdays—can be especially hard when you are in grief.

- These are times you may want to plan ahead for. Perhaps you could take a day off work on the anniversary of the death. Maybe on the next birthday of the parent who died you could visit the cemetery or scattering site.

- Many adult children whose parent has died find their own birthdays particularly difficult. After all, your birthday is the anniversary of the day your parent gave you life. Your parent may have also honored your birthday each year with much love and celebration. Now that your parent has died, no one will remember your birthday in the same way.

- Reach out to others on these difficult days. Talk about your feelings with a close friend.

CARPE DIEM

What's the next anniversary you've been dreading?
Make a plan right now for what you will do on that
day. Enlist a friend's help so you won't be alone.

45.

TAKE GOOD CARE OF YOURSELF

- Good self-care is nurturing and necessary for mourners, yet it's something many of us completely overlook.

- Try very hard to eat well and get adequate rest. Lay your body down 2-3 times a day for 20-30 minutes, even if you don't sleep. I know— you probably don't care very much about eating well right now, and you may be sleeping poorly. But taking care of yourself is truly one way to fuel healing and to begin to embrace life again.

- Drink at least 5-6 glasses of water each day. Dehydration can compound feelings of fatigue and disorientation.

- Exercise not only provides you with more energy, it can give you focused thinking time. Take a 20-minute walk every day. Or, if that seems too much, a five-minute walk. But don't over-exercise, because your body needs extra rest, as well.

- Now more than ever, you need to allow time for you.

CARPE DIEM

Are you taking a multi-vitamin? If not, now
is probably a good time to start.

46.

UNDERSTAND THE ROLE
OF "LINKING OBJECTS"

- You may be comforted by physical objects associated with the parent who died. It is not unusual for mourners to save clothing, jewelry, books, locks of hair and other personal items.

- Such "linking objects" may help you remember your parent and honor the life that was lived. Such objects may help you heal.

- Never think that being attached to these objects is morbid or wrong.

- Never hurry into disposing of the personal effects of your parent. You may want to leave some personal items untouched for months or sometimes years. This is OK as long as the objects offer comfort and don't inhibit healing.

- If you must dispose of your parent's estate quickly, try to do it with a sense of perspective. Ask yourself: Which items hold meaning for me? Which items will help me keep my memories alive? Try not to fall into the trap of making such decisions based on financial criteria.

CARPE DIEM

When and only when you're ready, ask a friend or family
member to help you sort through your parent's personal effects.
Sometimes it's good for siblings to take care of this task together.
Fill a memory box with significant objects and mementos.

47.

KEEP A JOURNAL

• Journals are an ideal way for some mourners to record thoughts and feelings.

• Remember—your inner thoughts and feelings about the death of your parent need to be expressed outwardly (which includes writing) if you are to heal.

• Consider jotting down your thoughts and feelings each night before you go to sleep. Your journal entries can be as long or as short as you want. Don't worry about your vocabulary, sentence structure, punctuation, etc. The important thing is to express what's going on inside.

• Or keep a dream journal, instead. Keep a blank book in your nightstand for recording your dreams when you wake up.

• If you're not a writer, consider talking your thoughts and feelings into a tape recorder. Your audio journal might allow you to say things you otherwise might not say. And replaying your journal entries in the months and years that follow might help you recognize your progress and growth.

CARPE DIEM

Stop by your local bookstore and choose a blank book you like the look and feel of. Visit a park on your way home and write your first entry.

48.

ORGANIZE A TREE PLANTING

- Trees represent the beauty, vibrancy and continuity of life.

- A specially planted and located tree can honor your parent and serves as a perennial memorial.

- You might write a short ceremony for the tree planting. (Or ask another family member to write one.) Consider a personalized metal marker or sign, too.

- For a more private option, plant a tree in your own yard. Consult your local nursery for an appropriate selection. Flowering trees are especially beautiful in the spring. You might also consider a variety of tree that your parent loved or that reminds you of the family home in which your parent raised you.

- This past Father's Day, I planted a tree in my yard in memory of my father. Some special friends gave me this tree for just this purpose.

CARPE DIEM

Order a tree for your own yard and plant it in honor of
the parent who died. You'll probably need someone
to help you prepare the hole and place the tree.

49.

PLAN A CEREMONY

- When words are inadequate, have ceremony.

- Ceremony assists in reality, recall, support, expression, transcendence.

- When personalized, the funeral ceremony can be a healing ritual. But ceremonies that take place later on can also be very meaningful.

- The ceremony might center on memories of your parent, "meaning of life" thoughts and feelings or affirmation of faith.

- Our culture doesn't always understand the value of ceremony. Don't expect that everyone around you will understand your desire to make use of ritual. However, don't allow their lack of understanding to persuade you to forego ceremonies both at the time of the death and months and years into the future.

CARPE DIEM

Hold a candle-lighting memory ceremony. Invite a small group of friends. Form a circle around a center candle, with each person holding their own small candle. Have each person light their memory candle and share a special memory of your parent. At the end, play a song or read a poem or prayer in memory of the parent who died.

50.

ORGANIZE A MEMORY BOOK

- Assembling a scrapbook that holds treasured photos and mementos of your parent can be a very healing activity.

- You might consider including a birth certificate, newspaper clippings, locks of hair, old letters—anything that helps capture the life of your parent or seems meaningful to you.

- Phone others who loved your parent and ask them to write a note or contribute photos.

- Other ideas: a memory box, a memory quilt, a personalized website. Find a seamstress who can turn an old shirt or blouse of your parent's into a stuffed animal. These can make wonderful "linking objects," even for us grown-ups!

- I have a special photo of my dad when he was three years old on display in my Center for Loss. One person asked me if I was creating a shrine (a term we often use inappropriately) and I said, "No, I've created a temple. Allow me to tell you about my precious father!"

CARPE DIEM

Buy an appropriate scrapbook or keepsake box today. Don't forget to buy the associated materials you'll need, such as photo pages or photo corners, glue, scissors, etc.

51.

DO A FAMILY HISTORY PROJECT

- For many adult children, the death of a parent arouses curiosity about the past. What was the parent's life like? Where did the grandparents and great-parents live?

- It's too late to ask your parent these questions, but if you have a surviving parent, now's the time. If both your parents have died, perhaps relatives or friends from their generation are available. Often they're happy to tell stories and fill in information gaps.

- You might find a greater need to connect to your extended family at this time. Do you have aunts and uncles, cousins, great aunts and uncles, etc. whom you don't know but would like to?

- While you may not have the desire to complete a thorough genealogy, you may be interested in gathering photos and stories. Audio- or video your elders as they talk about their past. Listen and learn.

- The year before he died, I did a one-hour video interview with my father. I used the book *The Mom and Dad Conversation Piece* by Bret Nicholaus and Paul Lowrie (Ballantine Books, 1997) as a source of questions. This video, in which he shares many details of his life, has become one of my most prized possessions.

CARPE DIEM

Assemble a photo album of your parent's life. Include photos from her childhood, young adult years, family life, etc. Try to find images that represent all the people and places that were special to her. When you're finished, have copies of the album made for each of your siblings.

52.

SUBSCRIBE TO HEALING

- There are a number of healing magazines for mourners. Most include mourner's stories of loss and renewed hope, poetry, meaningful artwork.

- Two of this author's favorites are *Living with Loss* (www.livingwithloss.com or 888-604-4673) and *Grief Digest* (www.centering.org or 866-218-0101). Both of these compassionate resources are filled with personal stories of loss and healing, grief education, poetry, etc.

- Instead of a grief magazine, consider a magazine you've always wanted to read but have never allowed yourself the time to.

- My father and I always shared a love for baseball. Shortly after his death I subscribed to *Sports Illustrated*. As I peruse the pages and read about baseball, tennis and other sports we enjoyed together, I just smile and think of the joy our mutual love of athletics brought us.

CARPE DIEM

Start a subscription today.

53.

DON'T BE CAUGHT OFF GUARD BY "GRIEFBURSTS"

- Sometimes heightened periods of sadness overwhelm mourners. These times can seem to come of out nowhere and can be frightening and painful.

- Even long after the death, something as simple as a sound, a smell or a phrase that reminds you of your parent can bring on a "griefburst."

- Allow yourself to experience griefbursts without shame or self-judgment, no matter where and when they occur. If you would feel more comfortable, retreat to somewhere private when these strong feelings surface.

- My dad listened to Frank Sinatra and the "Big Bands" during my growing up years. When I hear this music, I feel "sappy"—sad and happy all at the same time. At first it was painful to hear this music. Now I purposely play it sometimes. It helps me feel close to my dad and I know he is smiling down from heaven.

CARPE DIEM

Create an action plan for your next griefburst. For example, you might plan to drop whatever you are doing and go for a walk or record thoughts in your journal.

54.

THINK YOUNG

- It is the nature of children to live for the moment and appreciate today. All of us would benefit from a little more childlike wonder.

- Do something childish—blow bubbles, skip rope, visit a toy store, build a sand castle, fly a kite, climb a tree.

- If kids aren't already a part of your life, make arrangements to spend some time with them. Volunteer at a local school. Take a friend's children to the park one afternoon.

- What special memories do you cherish from your childhood? Was there something you and your parent liked to do together? Maybe you could do the same activity with your own children.

CARPE DIEM

Buy a gift for a child today just because.

55.

FOLLOW YOUR NOSE

- For centuries people have understood that certain smells induce certain feelings. Aromatherapy is the contemporary term for this age-old practice.

- Some comforting, memory-inducing smells include baby powder, freshly cut grass, dill, oranges, leather, lilacs.

- Essential oils, available at your local drugstore or bath and body shop, can be added to bath water or dabbed lightly on pulse points.

- Lavender relaxes. Rosewood and bergamot together lift the spirits. Peppermint invigorates. Chamomile and lavender are sleep aids.

CARPE DIEM

Visit a local bath and body shop and choose one or two essential oils or scented candles. Try using them today.

56.

LISTEN TO THE MUSIC

- Music can be very healing to mourners because it helps us access our feelings, both happy and sad. Music can soothe the spirit and nurture the heart.

- All types of music can be healing—rock & roll, classical, blues, folk.

- Consider listening to music you normally don't, perhaps the opera or the symphony. Or make a recording of your favorite songs, all together on one tape.

- Do you play an instrument or sing? Allow yourself the time to try these activities again soon.

- In honor of my dad, I bought a complete collection of Frank Sinatra music. Do you have a similar way to honor and remember your mom or dad?

CARPE DIEM

Visit a music store today and sample a few CDs or cassettes.
Buy yourself the one that moves you the most.

57.

PRAY

- Prayer is a way of communicating your innermost thoughts and feelings to the powers of the universe. As such, prayer is a form of mourning. And studies have shown that prayer can actually help people heal.

- If you believe in a higher power, pray. Pray for your parent who died. Pray for your questions about life and death to be answered. Pray for the strength to embrace your pain and to heal over time. Pray for others affected by this death.

- When you were a child, your parent may have taught you a simple prayer to say at bedtime. Do you remember it? Try adding it to your bedtime routine once again.

- Many places of worship have prayer lists. Call yours and ask that your name be added to the prayer list. On worship day, the whole congregation will pray for you. Often many individuals will pray at home for those on the prayer list, as well.

CARPE DIEM

Bow your head right now and say a silent prayer. If you are out of practice, don't worry; just let your thoughts flow naturally.

58.

LEARN SOMETHING NEW

- Sometimes mourners feel stuck. We can feel depressed and the daily routine of our lives can be joyless.

- Perhaps you would enjoy learning something new or trying a new hobby.

- What have you always wanted to learn but have never tried? Playing the guitar? Woodworking? Speaking French? Is there something your parent always wanted to learn to do but never did? Maybe you could learn on her behalf.

- Consider physical activities. Learning to play golf or doing karate have the added benefits of exercise.

- Some people like to try a hobby or activity their parent once enjoyed. This can be a way of giving tribute to your parent and feeling close to her at the same time.

CARPE DIEM

Get ahold of your local community calendar and sign up
for a class in something you have never tried before.

59.

TAKE A RISK

- For some, activities that harbor risk, real or perceived, are invigorating and life-affirming.

- Sometimes people who've encountered death, in particular, feel ready to try limit-stretching activities.

- Some ideas: hang-gliding, bungee jumping, skydiving, rock climbing.

- Don't confuse appropriate risk-taking with self-destructiveness. Never test your own mortality through inappropriate behaviors or inadequate safeguards.

CARPE DIEM

Schedule a sunrise hot air balloon ride with a trained, licensed balloonist. Toast the dawn with champagne at 2,000 feet.

60.

PICTURE THIS

- The visual arts have a way of making us see the world anew.

- Perhaps you would enjoy a visit to an art gallery or museum, a sculpture garden, a photography exhibit.

- Why not try to create some art yourself? Attend a watercolor or calligraphy class.

- Making pottery is something almost everyone enjoys. It's tactile and messy and whimsical. Or you could visit a ceramics shop and simply paint pottery that's already been made.

CARPE DIEM

Buy some paints, some brushes and a canvas and paint your feelings about the death. Don't worry about your artistic abilities; just let your imagination take charge.

61.

VOLUNTEER

- Consider honoring your parent's death through social activism. If she died of heart disease, collect money for the American Heart Association. If he had multiple sclerosis, walk in the annual MS walk nearest you.

- My father died from malignant melanoma (the deadliest form of skin cancer). I help sponsor an annual run/walk in my community that raises money to help combat this horrible disease. The contribution I make every year helps me remember my dad and feel like I'm helping prevent similar deaths in the future.

- Volunteer at a senior center, an elementary school, a local hospital— someplace befitting the parent who died.

- If your schedule is too hectic, offer money instead of time. Make your donation in memory of your parent.

CARPE DIEM

Call your local United Way and ask for some suggestions
about upcoming events you could participate in.

62.

VISIT THE GREAT OUTDOORS

- For many people it is restorative and energizing to spend time outside.

- Mourners often find nature's timeless beauty healing. The sound of a bird singing or the awesome presence of an old tree can help put things in perspective.

- Go on a nature walk. Or camping. Or canoeing. The farther away from civilization the better. Mother Earth knows more about kicking back than all the stress management experts on the planet—and she charges far less.

- When I'm missing my dad, I like to walk through cornfields. I grew up in Indiana and I have memories of being with my dad in or around cornfields. When I have a chance, I like to walk into a tall field of corn. The air wafting through the stalks and the smell of the corn reminds me of my childhood and my dad. Time seems to slow. Perhaps it actually does.

CARPE DIEM

Call your area forest service for a map of nearby walking or hiking trails. Take a hike sometime this week.

63.

SURF THE WEB

- The World Wide Web has a number of interesting and informative resources for mourners.

- Many articles about grief are available online. Books can also be purchased online. Most grief organizations now have Web pages. Children of Aging Parents might be a good place for you to start. Visit their website at www.caps4caregivers.org or call them at 1-800-227-7294.

- Search the words "grief" and "parent died" and see what you find. You may find a chatroom or message board with helpful stories and support from other adult children whose parents have died.

- Consider setting up your own website and telling your grief story online. You could also use this forum to memorialize your parent. Personal story websites like these can be poignant and healing both for the poster and the visitor.

CARPE DIEM

Sit down at your computer today and do a search. If you don't own a computer or have access to one at work, visit your local library. Don't forget to visit the Center for Loss website: www.centerforloss.com.

64.

WATCH FOR WARNING SIGNS

- Sometimes mourners fall back on self-destructive behaviors to get through this difficult time.

- Try to be honest with yourself about drug or alcohol abuse. Any kind of addictive behavior that is ultimately self-destructive can be a "red flag" that you need to get some help with your grief. This might include use of drugs or alcohol, gambling, extramarital affairs or difficulties in your work and personal relationships. If you're in over your head, ask someone for help.

- Are you having suicidal thoughts and feelings? Are you isolating yourself too much? Talk to someone today. Let people know you are hurting. They can't read your mind or open your heart.

CARPE DIEM

Acknowledging to ourselves that we have a problem may come too late. If someone suggests that you need help, consider yourself lucky to be so well-loved and get help immediately.

65.

SIMPLIFY YOUR LIFE

- Many of us today are taking stock of what's really important in our lives and trying to discard the rest.

- Mourners are often overwhelmed by all the tasks and commitments we have. If you can rid yourself of some of those extraneous burdens, you'll have more time for mourning and healing.

- What is it that is overburdening you right now? Have your name taken off junk mail lists, ignore your dirty house, stop attending any optional meetings you don't look forward to.

CARPE DIEM

Cancel your newspaper subscription(s) if you're depressed
by what you read. Quit watching TV news for a while.

66.

ESTABLISH A MEMORIAL FUND IN THE NAME OF THE PARENT WHO DIED

- Sometimes bereaved families ask that memorial contributions be made to specified charities in the name of the person who died. This practice allows friends and family members to show their support while helping the family feel that something good came of the death.

- You can establish a personalized and ongoing memorial to your parent.

- What was meaningful to your mother or father? Did she support a certain nonprofit or participate in a certain recreational activity? Was he politically active or affected by a certain illness?

- Your local bank or funeral home may have ideas about how to go about setting up a memorial fund.

CARPE DIEM

Call a sibling or family member and together brainstorm a list of ideas for a memorial. Suggest that both of you commit to making at least one additional phone call for information before the day is out.

67.

OR CHOOSE TO MEMORIALIZE YOUR PARENT IN OTHER SPECIAL WAYS

- Setting up a memorial fund is just one way to honor the life of your parent. Your family may come up with many other creative ideas.

- Consider your parent's loves and passions. If he were still here, what would make him proud to have his name associated with?

- Some families have set up scholarship funds. Some have donated books to the library or schools. Some have donated park benches or picnic tables, inscribed with an appropriate plaque. Some have planted gardens.

- You might also choose to carry on with something your parent loved to do or left unfinished.

- My dad loved his church. He always said he was a "good Methodist." In his absence, my mother (while not as devout as my father) has continued to give money and provide support to the church. (Besides—I fear my dad would come get us if we didn't keep making these contributions he found so important!)

CARPE DIEM

Ask yourself: What did my parent really love in life? What was most important to her? How can I keep this love alive?

68.

PREPARE YOURSELF FOR THE HOLIDAYS

- Because your parent is no longer there to share the holidays with, you may feel particularly sad and vulnerable during Christmas, Easter and other holidays.

- Each holiday has its own history for your family, a history that extends back in time to your childhood and even your parent's childhood. Your family's holiday traditions were formed decades, sometimes centuries, ago and resonate with layer upon layer of memories.

- You probably remember many of the things your parent did or said each holiday, and even memories may now feel painful. Over time, you will come to appreciate your holiday memories again. I'll always remember the Christmas my dad made footsteps from newspaper that led me downstairs to discover the neatest toy train, all set up and ready to go.

- Don't overextend yourself during the holidays. Don't feel you have to shop, bake, entertain, send cards, etc. if you're not up for it.

- Sometimes old holiday rituals are comforting after a death and sometimes they're not. Continue them only if they feel good to you; consider creating new ones, as well.

- My dad spent a number of Christmases with me and my family in the years just prior to his death. It was a ritual we looked forward to all year long. While we still enjoy the holidays, they aren't the same without Dad/Grandpa. Besides, he always helped do the dishes and that impressed my wife!

CARPE DIEM

What's the next major holiday? Make a game plan right now and let those you usually spend the day with know of your plan well in advance.

69.

FIND A GRIEF "BUDDY"

- Though no one else will grieve this death just like you, there are often many others who have had similar experiences. We are rarely totally alone on the path of mourning. Even when there is no guide, there are fellow travelers.

- Find a grief "buddy"—someone who is also mourning the death of a parent, someone you can talk to, someone who also needs a companion in grief right now.

- Make a pact with your grief buddy to call each other whenever one of you needs to talk. Promise to listen without judgment. Commit to spending time together.

- You might arrange to meet once a week for breakfast or lunch with your grief buddy.

CARPE DIEM

Do you know someone who also needs support after the death of a parent? Call her and ask her out to lunch today. If it feels right, discuss the possibility of being grief buddies.

70.

FORGIVE YOUR PARENTS
THEIR SHORTCOMINGS

- It's been said that parenting is the most difficult job in the world. If you have children yourself, you'll probably agree. It's fatiguing, frustrating, and never-ending.

- Like most people, your parents were probably far from perfect. But they undertook the Herculean task of parenting in the best way they could. As Maya Angelou wrote, "You did what you knew how to do and when you knew better, you did better."

- Whether you think your mother and father were wonderful parents or lousy ones—or a mixture of both, they loved you and you loved them. Maybe that's what counts most.

- Forgiveness doesn't mean saying that no wrong was done. It means acknowledging that mistakes were made but loving and honoring despite it all.

- Of course, victims of abuse may not be able to (and shouldn't automatically be expected to) forgive. In these cases, seeing a professional therapist may help you reconcile old hurts.

CARPE DIEM

Get a stack of 3x5 cards. On each card, write down one memory or aspect of your parent's personality that hurt you. When you're finished, tear up each card while saying aloud, "Mom/Dad, I forgive you for _____."

71.

IGNORE HURTFUL ADVICE

- Sometimes well-intended but misinformed friends will hurt you unknowingly with their words.

- You may be told:
    - I know how you feel.
    - Get on with your life.
    - Keep your chin up.
    - This is a blessing.
    - Your mother/father lived a long, full life.
    - Think of all you have to be thankful for.
    - He/she wouldn't want you to be sad.
    - Time heals all wounds.
    - You're strong. You'll get over it.

- Don't take this advice to heart. Such clichés are often offered because people don't know what else to say. The problem is, phrases like these diminish your unique and significant loss.

CARPE DIEM

Consider the clichés you've spoken to mourners in
the past in an attempt to comfort them. Forgive
yourself just as you should forgive your friends.

72.

MAKE A LIST OF GOALS

- While you should not set a particular time and course for your healing, it may help you to have made other life goals for the coming year.

- Make a list of short-term goals for the next three months. Perhaps some of the goals could have to do with mourning activities (e.g. make a memory book).

- Also make a list of long-term goals for the next year. Be both realistic and compassionate with yourself as you consider what's feasible and feels good and what will only add too much stress to your life.

CARPE DIEM

Write a list of goals for this week. Your goals may be as simple as: Go to work every day. Tell John I love him once a day. Take a walk on Tuesday night.

73.

COUNT YOUR BLESSINGS

- You may not be feeling very good about your life right now. That's OK. There is, indeed, a time for every purpose under heaven.

- Still, you are blessed. Your life has purpose and meaning. It will just take you some time to think and feel this through for yourself.

- Think of all you have to be thankful for. This is not to deny the hurt, for the hurt needs to take precedence right now. But it may help to consider the things that make your life worth living, too.

CARPE DIEM

If you're feeling ready, make a list of the blessings in your life:
your family, your friends, your job, your house. Be specific. "I'm
thankful for John's smile. My Wenlock roses. The way the
sun slants through my kitchen window in the morning."

74.

DO SOMETHING YOU'RE GOOD AT

- Often it helps mourners to affirm their worth to others and to themselves.

- Do something you're good at! Ride a bike. Bake a cake. Do the crossword puzzle. Write a poem. Play with your kids. Talk to a friend.

- Have other people told you you're good at this or that? Next time you're complimented in this way, take it to heart! Embrace your gifts that are God-given.

CARPE DIEM

Make a list of ten things you're good at. Do one of them today and afterwards, reflect on how you feel.

75.

IMAGINE YOUR PARENT IN HEAVEN

- Do you believe in an afterlife? Do you hope that your parent still exists in some way?

- Most mourners I've talked to—and that number runs into the tens of thousands—are comforted by a belief or a hope that somehow, somewhere, their parent lives on in health and happiness. For some, this belief is grounded in religious faith. For others it is simply a spiritual sense.

- The belief that their parents live on helps some adult children reconcile their feelings of orphanhood. After all, if your parent is watching over you from heaven, isn't he still, in some way, parenting you?

- Some adult children have dreams in which their parent seems to be communicating with them. Some feel the overwhelming presence of their parent on occasion. Some actually "see" or "hear" their parent. These are common, normal experiences and are often quite comforting.

- For me, going out into nature helps me quiet myself in ways that help me feel in communication with my dad. Just the other day my youngest child, Jaimie, and I were out on the deck in the dark. She looked up at the night sky and said, "Daddy, sometimes when I look up in the sky I think about Grandpa." I'm sure that made my dad smile down on us from above.

CARPE DIEM

If you believe in heaven, close your eyes and imagine what it might be like. Imagine your parent strong and smiling. Imagine him doing what he loves to do in the company of loved ones who have gone before him.

76.

PRACTICE BREATHING IN AND OUT

- After a parent dies, sometimes what we need most is just to "be." In our goal-oriented society, many of us have lost the knack for simply living.

- Drop all your plans and obligations for today and do nothing.

- Meditate if meditation helps center you. Meditation is simply quiet, relaxed contemplation. You needn't follow any particular rules or techniques. Simply find a quiet place where you can think without distraction and rid your mind of superficial thoughts and concerns. Be still, close your eyes and focus on breathing in and out. Relax your muscles. Listen to your own heartbeat.

CARPE DIEM

Try reflecting on this thought: "As I allow myself to mourn, I create an opening in my heart. Releasing the tensions of grief, surrendering to the struggle, means freeing myself to go forward."

77.

TALK OUT LOUD TO THE PARENT WHO DIED

- Sometimes it feels good to talk to your parent. Pretend he's sitting in the chair across from you and tell him how you're doing.

- Talk to photos of your parent. Share your deepest thoughts and feelings with her. Make it part of your daily routine to say "Good morning!" to that photo on your nightstand. (Just be careful who's in earshot! Ha-ha!)

- Visit the cemetery (or columbarium or scattering place if your parent was cremated) and if you're not too self-conscious, talk to your mother or father.

- Keep symbols of your parent around, such as photos or personal belongings that help connect you with the parent who died. They also help activate your need to mourn.

CARPE DIEM

If you haven't already, put a photo of your parent in your wallet or purse. Look at it and maybe even talk to it when you're really missing your mom or dad.

78.

DRAW A "GRIEF MAP"

- The death of your parent may have stirred up all kinds of thoughts and feelings inside you. These thoughts and feelings may seem overwhelming or even "crazy."

- Rest assured that you're not crazy, you're grieving. Your thoughts and feelings—no matter how scary or strange they seem to you—are normal and necessary.

- Sometimes, corralling all your varied thoughts and feelings in one place can make them feel more manageable. You could write about them, but you can also draw them out in diagram form.

- Make a large circle at the center of your map and label it GRIEF. This circle represents your thoughts and feeling since the death. Now draw lines radiating out of this circle and label each line with a thought or feeling that has contributed to your grief. For example, you might write GUILT in a bubble at the end of one line. Next to the word guilt, jot down notes about why you feel guilty.

- Your grief map needn't look pretty or follow any certain rules. The most important thing is the process of creating it. When you're finished, explain it to someone who cares about you.

CARPE DIEM

Stop by your local art supply or hobby shop today and
pick up a large piece of poster board or banner paper. Set
aside an hour or so to work on your grief map today.

79.

SET ASIDE THE ANNIVERSARY OF THE DEATH AS A HOLIDAY

- Perhaps you dread the anniversary of your parent's death. Many adult children feel particularly sad and helpless on this day.

- Consider setting aside the anniversary as an annual holiday. Each year, visit your parent's grave or scattering site. Or plan a ritual activity, such as going on a hike or hosting a family dinner. Perhaps plan a ceremony with friends and family.

- Commemorate the life that was lived by doing something your parent would have appreciated.

- You might want to spend this day in the company of others who love you.

CARPE DIEM

Call your siblings or others who loved your parent and plan an activity for the anniversary of the death.

80.

TALK TO A COUNSELOR

- While grief counseling is not for everyone, many mourners are helped through their grief journeys by a compassionate counselor. It's not indulgent or crazy to see a counselor after a parent dies—it's simply good self-care!

- If possible, find a counselor who has experience with grief and loss issues.

- Ask your friends for referrals to a counselor they've been helped by.

- Your religious leader may also be a good person to talk to during this time, but only if she affirms your need to mourn this death and search for meaning.

CARPE DIEM

Schedule an initial interview with at least two counselors
so you can see whom you're most comfortable with.

81.

LOOK INTO SUPPORT GROUPS

- Grief support groups are a healing, safe place for many mourners to express their thoughts and feelings. Sharing similar experiences with others who have lost a parent may help you feel like you're not alone, that you're not going crazy.

- Support groups give you a time and a place—as well as permission— to mourn. They can also help you assess the relationship you had with your parent and consider the ways in which the death has changed you. Finally, support groups provide you with ideas and choices for reconciling your grief.

- Your local hospice or funeral home may offer a free or low-cost support group. If you have several friends whose parents have died, you might also ask these friends if they would like to get together and talk about their grief journeys.

- If you are newly bereaved, you may not feel ready for a support group. Many mourners are more open to joining a support group 6-9 months after the death. Do what feels right for you.

CARPE DIEM

Call around today for support group information. If you're feeling ready, plan to attend a meeting this week or next.

82.

HELP OTHERS

- Help others! But I'm the one who needs help right now, you may be thinking.

- It's true, you do deserve special compassion and attention right now. But often, people find healing in selflessness.

- Consider volunteering at a nursing home, a homeless shelter, your neighborhood school. Do something your mom or dad would have appreciated.

- If you're well into your grief journey, you may find yourself ready and able to help other mourners by starting a support group or volunteering at a hospice.

- You might even want to plan a trip to my Center for Loss and Life Transition and attend my small group retreat on "Comprehensive Bereavement Skills Training." I'll leave the light on for you! (Call us at (970) 226-6050 and we'll send you a brochure and application.)

CARPE DIEM

Do something nice for someone else today, maybe
someone who doesn't really deserve it.

83.

TAKE YOUR PHONE OFF THE HOOK AND UNPLUG THE COMPUTER

- In our hectic lives, the phone is both a can't-live-without-it convenience and an annoying interruption.

- Sometimes we use the phone or e-mail when we should be talking face-to-face.

- Next time you have an urge to call a friend, drop by and visit him instead. Notice how much more intimate and healing it can be to converse in person.

- Don't hide out from yourself or others through the use of any technology. As the Swiss writer Max Frisch has observed, "Technology is the knack of so arranging the world that we do not have to experience it."

CARPE DIEM

Take your phone off the hook tonight (or turn the ringer off). Don't review your messages until tomorrow.

84.

SAY NO

- Especially soon after the death of your parent, you may lack the energy as well as the desire to participate in activities you used to enjoy. The fancy term for this is "anhedonia," which is the lack of ability to experience pleasure in things you previously found pleasurable. (Next time someone asks how you're doing, just say, "Oh, I'm feeling a bit anhedonistic today" and watch the response you get!)

- It's OK to say no when you're asked to help with a project or attend a party.

- Write a note to the people who've invited you and explain your feelings. Be sure to thank them for the invitation.

- Realize that you can't keep saying no forever. There will always be that first family reunion, birthday party, holiday dinner, etc. Don't miss out on life's most joyful celebrations.

CARPE DIEM

Say no to something today. Allow yourself not to feel guilty about it.

85.

TAKE A MINI-VACATION

- Don't have time to take time off? Plan several mini-vacations this month instead.

- What creative ideas can you come up with to renew yourself? Here are a few ideas to get you started.
    - Schedule a massage with a professional massage therapist
    - Have a spiritual growth weekend. Retreat into nature. Plan some alone time.
    - Go for a drive with no particular destination in mind. Explore the countryside, slow down and observe what you see.
    - Treat yourself to a night in a hotel or bed and breakfast.
    - Visit a museum or a zoo.
    - Go to a yard sale or auction.
    - Go rollerskating or rollerblading with a friend.
    - Drop by a health food store and walk the aisles.

CARPE DIEM

Plan a mini-vacation for today. Spend one
hour doing something special.

86.

RECONNECT WITH SOMEONE SPECIAL

- Throughout our lives, we often lose contact with people who've touched us or made a difference somehow.

- Death can make us realize that keeping in touch with these people is well worth the effort.

- Whom have you loved or admired but haven't spoken with for a long time?

- Consider teachers, old lovers, childhood friends, past neighbors. Also consider friends and family from your parent's generation. Often older people lead slower, more lonely lives and are touchingly appreciative when a younger person takes the time to visit or remember them.

CARPE DIEM

Write a letter to someone you haven't been in touch with
for a long time. Track down her address and phone
number. Catch her up on your life and invite her to do
the same by calling you or writing you back.

87.

EAT COMFORT FOOD

- Comfort food is food that makes you feel safe, loved, at home; it's often associated with foods we ate as children.

- Some examples: macaroni and cheese, mashed potatoes, chicken soup, hot cocoa laden with tiny marshmallows.

- What foods make you feel this way? What foods did your parent prepare for you that will always remind you of her love? When you were a child, what was your favorite dinner?

- My dad and I shared a love for spaghetti. Did you have a favorite food you and your parent both enjoyed?

CARPE DIEM

Tonight, in honor of your parent, prepare your favorite childhood meal for your family. If they live nearby, invite your siblings to join you.

88.

REMEMBER OTHERS WHO
HAD A SPECIAL RELATIONSHIP
WITH YOUR PARENT

- At times your appropriately inward focus will make you feel alone in your grief. But you're not alone. There are probably many other people who loved and miss your parent.

- Think about others who were affected by your parent's death: friends, neighbors, distant relatives, grandchildren.

- Is there someone outside of the primary "circle of mourners" who may be struggling with this death? Perhaps you could call her and offer your condolences.

CARPE DIEM

Today, write and mail a brief supportive note to
someone else affected by the death. If you aren't a
writer, give them a call or stop in for a visit.

89.

SCHEDULE SOMETHING THAT GIVES YOU PLEASURE EACH AND EVERY DAY

• Often mourners need something to look forward to, a reason to get out of bed today.

• It's hard to look forward to each day when you know you will be experiencing pain and sadness.

• To counterbalance your normal and necessary mourning, plan something you enjoy doing every day.

• Reading, baking, going for a walk, having lunch with a friend, gardening, playing computer games—whatever brings you enjoyment.

CARPE DIEM

What's on tap for today? Squeeze in something you
enjoy, no matter how hectic your schedule.

90.

TEACH OTHERS ABOUT GRIEF AND MOURNING

- To love is to one day mourn. You have learned this most poignant of life's lessons.

- Maybe you could teach what you are learning to others. Tell your friends and family about the six needs of mourning. Teach them how they can best support you.

- Teach your children about mourning and help them mourn the death of their grandparent. Provide them with mourning opportunities and activities. Model your own grief and mourning openly and honestly. Whatever you do, don't hide your grief in an effort to protect your children. This will teach them to hide their feelings, too.

- Share your wisdom in the safety of a grief support group.

- Remember that each person's grief is unique. Your experiences will not be shared or appreciated by everyone.

CARPE DIEM

Buy a friend the companion book to this one, called *Healing A Friend's Grieving Heart: 100 Practical Ideas for Helping Someone You Love Through Loss*. It provides concise grief education and practical tips for helping.

91.

SPEND TIME ALONE

- Reaching out to others while we're in mourning is necessary. Mourning is hard work and you can't get through it by yourself.

- Still, you will also need alone time as you work on the six needs of mourning. To slow down and to turn inward, you must sometimes insist on solitude.

- Schedule alone time into each week. Go for a walk in the woods. Lock your bedroom door and read a book. Work in your garden.

- Don't shut your friends and family out altogether, but do heed the call for contemplative silence.

CARPE DIEM

Schedule one hour of solitude into your day today.

92.

CREATE A SANCTUARY JUST FOR YOU

- Mourners need safe places they can go when they feel ready to embrace their grief.

- Create a sanctuary in your own home, a retreat that's just for you. Furnish it with a comfy chair, reading materials, a journal, a stereo with appropriate CDs or cassettes. No TV. Or, you may want this to be a room dedicated to silence. As Thomas Moore has noted, "Silence allows many sounds to reach awareness that otherwise would be unheard."

- An outside "room" can be equally effective. Do you have a porch or patio where you can just "be"? Locate a comfortable chair and install a table-top fountain.

- Your sanctuary, even if just a simple room, can become a place dedicated exclusively to the needs of the soul. The death of your parent requires "soul work." Your creation of a sanctuary honors that reality.

CARPE DIEM

Identify a spot in your house that can be your
sanctuary. Begin readying it today.

93.

SLEEP TIGHT

- Mourning is fatiguing work. Feelings of exhaustion and low energy are extremely common.

- Your body is telling you it needs rest, so indulge your fatigue. Schedule at least eight hours of slumber into your day. Develop a relaxing bedtime routine so you're ready for sleep.

- Buy yourself new bedding and a good new pillow—or hang on to an old pillow that has always brought you comfort.

- Lie down for short rest periods periodically throughout the day. Take an afternoon nap if you feel like it.

- If you feel you are "oversleeping," see your doctor. Sometimes this can be a symptom of a more severe depression. I often say, "When in doubt, get checked out."

CARPE DIEM

Tonight, begin getting ready for bed right after dinner. Take your phone off the hook, bathe or shower, listen to soothing music, sip hot herbal tea in bed as you read a good book or write in your journal.

94.

VISIT THE CEMETERY

- Visiting the cemetery is an important mourning ritual. It helps us embrace our loss and remember our parent who died.

- Memorial Day, Veteran's Day, Labor Day, Mother's Day and Father's Day are traditional days to visit the cemetery and pay respects. You might also want to spend time at the gravesite on your mother's or father's birthday.

- If your parent's body was cremated, you may want to visit the scattering site or columbarium.

- Ask a friend or family member to go with you. You may feel comforted by their presence. On the other hand, you may find it more meaningful to go by yourself. At times, your aloneness may help you feel closer to your parent who died.

CARPE DIEM

If you can, drop by the cemetery today with a nosegay of fresh flowers. Scatter the petals over the grave.

95.

TAKE SOME TIME OFF WORK

- Typically, our society grants us three days "bereavement leave" and then expects us to return to work as if nothing happened.

- As you know, three days is a paltry allowance for grief. Talk to your supervisor about taking off some additional time following your parent's death. Some companies will grant extended leaves of absence or sabbaticals in some situations.

- If you simply can't take off additional time, request that your work load be lightened for the next several months.

- On the other hand, the routine of work comforts some mourners. Returning to work and to co-workers who care about you may be just what you need—so long as you're not overworking in an attempt— conscious or subconscious—to avoid your grief.

CARPE DIEM

Take a mental health day today and call in sick. Spend
the day resting or doing something you enjoy.

96.

LET GO OF DESTRUCTIVE MYTHS ABOUT GRIEF AND MOURNING

- Unknowingly, you have probably internalized many of our society's harmful myths about grief and mourning.

- Here are some to let go of:
  - I need to be strong and carry on.
  - Tears are a sign of weakness.
  - I need to get over my grief.
  - Death is something we don't talk about.

- Sometimes these myths will cause you to feel guilty about or ashamed of your true thoughts and feelings.

- Your grief is your grief. It's normal and necessary. Allow it to be what it is. Allow it to last as long as it lasts. Strive to be an authentic mourner—one who openly and honestly expresses what you think and feel.

CARPE DIEM

De-mythologize grief in your house by talking to your family about grief and mourning. Let them know that their feelings about your parent's death are normal and necessary. Share how you've been feeling.

97.

GET AWAY FROM IT ALL

- Sometimes it takes a change of scenery to reveal the texture of our lives.

- New people and places help us see our lives from a new vantage point and can assist us in our search for meaning.

- Often, getting away from it all means leaving civilization behind and retreating to nature. But it can also mean temporarily abandoning your environment and spending time in one that's altogether different.

- Visit a foreign country. Go backpacking in the wilderness. Spend a weekend at a monastery. Is there someplace your parent always dreamed of visiting but never did? Maybe you can travel there on his behalf.

- In the Bible, the career of Abraham begins with God saying, "Go forth." An alternative translation of the Hebrew is "Go to yourself." The practice of voluntary exile was actually designed to humble oneself and remind oneself that everything comes from God.

CARPE DIEM

Plan a trip to somewhere far away. Ask a friend to travel with you.

98.

REASSESS YOUR PRIORITIES

- Death has a way of making us rethink our lives and the meaningfulness of the ways we spend them.

- The death of a parent often challenges adult children to consider their own lives and deaths. You've witnessed a life come to an end. Was it a rich, loving, satisfying life? What can you learn from your parent's life and death?

- What gives your life meaning? What doesn't? Take steps to spend more of your time on the former and less on the latter.

- Now may be the time to reconfigure your life. Choose a satisfying new career. Go back to school. Begin volunteering. Move closer to your family. Be kinder and more compassionate.

CARPE DIEM

Imagine yourself five years from now. What is your life like?
How do you feel about the death of your parent? Is your future
what you hoped it would be? How can you begin to make
changes now so that your life will become what you wish?

99.

UNDERSTAND THE CONCEPT OF "RECONCILIATION"

- Sometimes you'll hear about mourners "recovering" from grief. This term is damaging because it implies that grief is an illness that must be cured. It also connotes a return to the way things were before the death.

- Mourners don't recover from grief. We become "reconciled" to it. In other words, we learn to live with it and are forever changed by it.

- This does not mean a life of misery, however. Mourners often not only heal but grow through grief. Our lives can potentially be deeper and more meaningful after the death of someone loved.

- Reconciliation takes time. You may not become truly reconciled to your loss for several years and even then will have "griefbursts" (see Idea 53) forever.

- I believe every human being wants to "mourn well" the death of a parent. It is as essential as breathing. Some people make the choice to give momentum to their mourning, while others deny or avoid it. The path you choose to take will make all the difference. Move toward your grief and go on to live until you die!

CARPE DIEM

Write down the following definition of reconciliation and post it somewhere you will see it often: It is not my goal to "get over" my grief. It is my goal to experience and express my grief and learn to live with it.

100.

BELIEVE IN YOUR CAPACITY TO HEAL AND GROW THROUGH GRIEF

- In time, you may find that you are growing emotionally and spiritually as a result of your grief journey.

- Many adult children have told me that their parents' deaths made them "grow up." They became more responsible, more mature and often more compassionate.

- Growth means a new inner balance with no end points. Your life will never be exactly the same as it was when your parent was still alive.

- Growth means exploring our assumptions about life. Ultimately, exploring our assumptions about life after the death of someone loved can make those assumptions richer and more life-affirming.

- Growth means utilizing our potentials. The encounter of grief reawakens us to the importance of utilizing our potentials—our capacities to mourn our losses openly and without shame, to be interpersonally effective in our relationships with others, and to continue to discover fulfillment in life, living and loving.

CARPE DIEM

Consider the ways in which you may be growing
since the death of your parent.

A FINAL WORD

I became a man the day my father died. Nothing in my life gave
me more clarity and a stronger sense of responsibility. I've become a
better lover, a closer friend and a kinder stranger.

—Matthew McConaughey

The death of my father has changed me in many ways. Perhaps
most of all, I have become more conscious of the responsibility
I have to my own three children to strive to be a gentle, loving,
compassionate father. While I understood this before, since
my father's death I more fully embrace this responsibility—this
opportunity.

The death of my father has taught me what it means to love my
children and make memories with them each and every day. As
my father's child, I can now say with complete surety that I make
memories with my own children by enjoying the simple things in
life: playing a game together, taking a vacation get-away, wrestling,
spraying each other with the hose, shooting hoops with my son,
watching my daughter perform in a play, having my seven-year-old
proudly tell me, "I'm going to be an artist when I grow up." Those
are the magic moments that will live in my heart forever.

The death of my father has taught me to slow down, to enjoy the
moment, to find hidden treasures everywhere. His death has invited
me to live fully in the present while I remember my past and
embrace my future. Yes, grief awakens us to a new sense of time!

The death of my father has taught me to seek a sense of belonging,
a sense of meaning, a sense of purpose both in my life's work and
in my relationships with family and friends. His death has reminded
me that there are miracles in loving and being loved.

The death of my father has also taught me that self-care is essential
as I experience the ebbs and flows of my journey into grief.

While I have learned to accept outside support, I've also learned about self-acceptance. Practicing self-care has helped me mourn authentically in ways that have helped me heal. While some people have tried to discuss or minimize my grief (after all, I am a grief counselor and write books about death and loss), I haven't let them. Regardless of how many books I write and workshops I teach, I must honor the need to mourn my father's death from deep in my soul.

Just one more thing: Right now, take a moment to close your eyes, open your heart and remember your parent's special smile.

Bless you. I hope we meet one day.

THE MOURNER'S CODE

Ten Self-Compassionate Principles

Though you should reach out to others as you journey through grief, you should not feel obligated to accept the unhelpful responses you may receive from some people. You are the one who is grieving, and as such, you have certain "rights" no one should try to take away from you.

The following list is intended both to empower you to heal and to decide how others can and cannot help. This is not to discourage you from reaching out to others for help, but rather to assist you in distinguishing useful responses from hurtful ones.

1. **You have the right to experience your own unique grief.** No one else will grieve in exactly the same way you do. So, when you turn to others for help, don't allow them to tell you what you should or should not be feeling.

2. **You have the right to talk about your grief.** Talking about your grief will help you heal. Seek out others who will allow you to talk as much as you want, as often as you want, about your grief. If at times you don't feel like talking, you also have the right to be silent.

3. **You have the right to feel a multitude of emotions.** Confusion, numbness, disorientation, fear, guilt and relief are just a few of the emotions you might feel as part of your grief journey. Others may try to tell you that feeling angry, for example, is wrong. Don't take these judgmental responses to heart. Instead, find listeners who will accept your feelings without condition.

4. **You have the right to be tolerant of your physical and emotional limits.** Your feelings of loss and sadness will probably leave you feeling fatigued. Respect what your body and mind are telling you. Get daily rest. Eat balanced meals.

And don't allow others to push you into doing things you don't feel ready to do.

5. **You have the right to experience "griefbursts."** Sometimes, out of nowhere, a powerful surge of grief may overcome you. This can be frightening, but it is normal and natural. Find someone who understands and will let you talk it out.

6. **You have the right to make use of ritual.** The funeral ritual does more than acknowledge the death of someone loved. It helps provide you with the support of caring people. More importantly, the funeral is a way for you to mourn. If others tell you the funeral or other healing rituals such as these are silly or unnecessary, don't listen.

7. **You have the right to embrace your spirituality.** If faith is a part of your life, express it in ways that seem appropriate to you. Allow yourself to be around people who understand and support your religious beliefs. If you feel angry at God, find someone to talk with who won't be critical of your feelings of hurt and abandonment.

8. **You have the right to search for meaning.** You may find yourself asking, "Why did he or she die? Why this way? Why now?" Some of your questions may have answers, but some may not. And watch out for the clichéd responses some people may give you. Comments like, "It was God's will" or "Think of what you have to be thankful for" are not helpful and you do not have to accept them.

9. **You have the right to treasure your memories.** Memories are one of the best legacies that exist after the death of someone loved. You will always remember. Instead of ignoring your memories, find others with whom you can share them.

10. **You have the right to move toward your grief and heal.** Reconciling your grief will not happen quickly. Remember, grief is a process, not an event. Be patient and tolerant with yourself and avoid people who are impatient and intolerant with you. Neither you nor those around you must forget that the death of someone loved changes your life forever.

SEND US YOUR IDEAS
FOR HEALING THE ADULT
CHILD'S GRIEVING HEART!

I'd love to hear you practical ideas for being self-compassionate in grief. I may use them in future editions of this book or in other publications through the Center for Loss. Please jot down your idea and mail it to:

Dr. Alan Wolfelt
The Center for Loss and Life Transition
3735 Broken Bow Rd.
Fort Collins, CO 80526
wolfelt@centerforloss.com

I look forward to hearing from you!

My idea:

_____

_____

_____

_____

_____

My name and mailing address:

_____

_____

_____

_____

ALSO BY ALAN WOLFELT

Understanding Your Grief
Ten Essential Touchstones for Finding Hope and Healing Your Heart

One of North America's leading grief educators, Dr. Alan Wolfelt has written many books about healing in grief. This book is his most comprehensive, covering the essential lessons that mourners have taught him in his three decades of working with the bereaved.

In compassionate, down-to-earth language, *Understanding Your Grief* describes ten touchstones—or trail markers—that are essential physical, emotional, cognitive, social, and spiritual signs for mourners to look for on their journey through grief.

The Ten Essential Touchstones:

1. Open to the presence of your loss.
2. Dispel misconceptions about grief.
3. Embrace the uniqueness of your grief.
4. Explore what you might experience.
5. Recognize you are not crazy.
6. Understand the six needs of mourning.
7. Nurture yourself.
8. Reach out for help.
9. Seek reconciliation, not resolution.
10. Appreciate your transformation.

Think of your grief as a wilderness—a vast, inhospitable forest. You must journey through this wilderness. To find your way out, you must become acquainted with its terrain and learn to follow the sometimes hard-to-find trail that leads to healing. In the wilderness of your grief, the touchstones are your trail markers. They are the signs that let you know you are on the right path. When you learn to identify and rely on the touchstones, you will find your way to hope and healing.

ISBN 978-1-879651-35-7 • 176 pages • softcover • $14.95

Companion
PRESS

All Dr. Wolfelt's publications can be ordered by mail from:
Companion Press
3735 Broken Bow Road
Fort Collins, CO 80526
(970) 226-6050
www.centerforloss.com

ALSO BY ALAN WOLFELT

The Understanding Your Grief Journal
Exploring the Ten Essential Touchstones

Writing can be a very effective form of mourning, or expressing your grief outside yourself. And it is through mourning that you heal in grief.

The Understanding Your Grief Journal is a companion workbook to Dr. Wolfelt's *Understanding Your Grief.* Designed to help mourners explore the many facets of their unique grief through journaling, this compassionate book interfaces with the ten essential touchstones. Throughout, journalers are asked specific questions about their own unique grief journeys as they relate to the touchstones and are provided with writing space for the many questions asked.

Purchased as a set together with *Understanding Your Grief,* this journal is a wonderful mourning tool and safe place for those in grief. It also makes an ideal grief support group workbook.

ISBN 978-1-879651-39-5 • 150 pages • softcover • $14.95

Companion
PRESS

All Dr. Wolfelt's publications can be ordered by mail from:
Companion Press
3735 Broken Bow Road
Fort Collins, CO 80526
(970) 226-6050
www.centerforloss.com

ALSO BY ALAN WOLFELT

The Wilderness of Grief
Finding Your Way

A beautiful, hardcover gift book version of
Understanding Your Grief

Understanding Your Grief provides a comprehensive exploration of grief and the ten essential touchstones for finding hope and healing your heart. *The Wilderness of Grief* is an excerpted version of *Understanding Your Grief*, making it approachable and appropriate for all mourners.

This concise book makes an excellent gift for anyone in mourning. On the book's inside front cover is room for writing an inscription to your grieving friend.

While some readers will appreciate the more in-depth *Understanding Your Grief*, others may feel overwhelmed by the amount of information it contains. For these readers we recommend *The Wilderness of Grief*. (Fans of *Understanding Your Grief* will also want a copy of *The Wilderness of Grief* to turn to in spare moments.)

The Wilderness of Grief is an ideal book for the bedside or coffee table. Pick it up before bed and read just a few pages. You'll be carried off to sleep by its gentle, affirming messages of hope and healing.

ISBN 978-1-879651-52-4 • 128 pages • hardcover • $15.95

Companion
PRESS

All Dr. Wolfelt's publications can be ordered by mail from:
Companion Press
3735 Broken Bow Road
Fort Collins, CO 80526
(970) 226-6050
www.centerforloss.com

ALSO BY ALAN WOLFELT

Living in the Shadow of the Ghosts of Grief
Step into the Light

Reconcile old losses and open the door to infinite joy and love

"Accumulated, unreconciled loss affects every aspect of our lives. Living in the Shadow is a beautifully written compass with the needle ever-pointing in the direction of hope."
— Greg Yoder, grief counselor

"So often we try to dance around our grief. This book offers the reader a safe place to do the healing work of "catch-up" mourning, opening the door to a life of freedom, authenticity and purpose."
— Kim Farris-Luke, bereavement coordinator

Are you depressed? Anxious? Angry? Do you have trouble with trust and intimacy? Do you feel a lack of meaning and purpose in your life? You may well be living in the shadow of the ghosts of grief.

When you suffer a loss of any kind—whether through abuse, divorce, job loss, the death of someone loved or other transitions, you naturally grieve inside. To heal your grief, you must express it. That is, you must mourn your grief. If you don't, you will carry your grief into your future, and it will undermine your happiness for the rest of your life.

This compassionate guide will help you learn to identify and mourn your carried grief so you can go on to live the joyful, whole life you deserve.

ISBN 978-1-879651-51-7 • 160 pages • softcover • $13.95

Companion

All Dr. Wolfelt's publications can be ordered by mail from:
Companion Press
3735 Broken Bow Road
Fort Collins, CO 80526
(970) 226-6050
www.centerforloss.com

ALSO BY ALAN WOLFELT

The Journey Through Grief
Reflections On Healing
Second Edition

This popular hardcover book makes a wonderful gift for those who grieve, helping them gently engage in the work of mourning. Comforting and nurturing, *The Journey Through Grief* doses mourners with the six needs of mourning, helping them soothe themselves at the same time it helps them heal.

Back by popular demand, we are now offering *The Journey Through Grief* again in hardcover. The hardcover version of this beautiful book makes a wonderful, healing gift for the newly bereaved.

This revised, second edition of *The Journey Through Grief* takes Dr. Wolfelt's popular book of reflections and adds space for guided journaling, asking readers thoughtful questions about their unique mourning needs and providing room to write responses.

The Journey Through Grief is organized around the six needs that all mourners must yield to—indeed embrace—if they are to go on to find continued meaning in life and living. Following a short explanation of each mourning need is a series of brief, spiritual passages that, when read slowly and reflectively, help mourners work through their unique thoughts and feelings. *The Journey Through Grief* is being used by many faith communities as part of their grief support programs.

ISBN 978-1-879651-11-1 • hardcover • 176 pages • $21.95

Companion

All Dr. Wolfelt's publications can be ordered by mail from:
Companion Press
3735 Broken Bow Road
Fort Collins, CO 80526
(970) 226-6050
www.centerforloss.com

CPSIA information can be obtained at www.ICGtesting.com
Printed in the USA
LVOW132038300812

296784LV00001B/6/P